C000173466

CONTENTS

FOREWORD

'TIS THE SEASON TO BE JOLLY' ✣ 5

Advent 6 ✣ *'Christ's Mass'* 7 ✣ *Noël* 8 ✣ *Xmas* 9 ✣ *Boxing Day* 10 ✣ *The Pantomime* 12 ✣ *The Twelve Days of Christmas* 13 ✣ *Twelfth Night* 15 ✣ *Epiphany* 16 ✣ *Christmas Parties and Paper Hats* 18 ✣ *Christmas Cards* 19 ✣

'DECK THE HALLS WITH BOUGHS OF HOLLY' ✣ 23

The Wreath 24 ✣ *Bells* 25 ✣ *The Nativity Scene* 26 ✣ *Holly* 27 ✣ *Kissing Under the Mistletoe* 28 ✣ *The Poinsettia* 30 ✣ *The Yule Log* 31 ✣

'O CHRISTMAS TREE, O CHRISTMAS TREE' ✣ 33

The Tree 34 ✣ *Candles* 38 ✣ *The Star* 39 ✣ *Tinsel* 41 ✣ *Baubles and Apples* 42 ✣ *Gifts* 43 ✣

'THE GOOSE IS GETTING FAT' ✣ 45

The Turkey 46 ✣ *The Pudding* 47 ✣ *'Firing' the Pudding* 48 ✣ *The Coin in the Pudding* 49 ✣ *Mince Pies* 51 ✣ *Christmas Cake* 52 ✣ *The Stollen* 52 ✣ *Crackers* 53 ✣

'HE SEES YOU WHEN YOU'RE SLEEPING' ✣ 55

Santa Claus 56 ✣ *The Sleigh and Reindeer* 58 ✣ *Father Christmas* 61 ✣ *Stockings* 62 ✣ *Why the Chimney?* 63 ✣

'TROLL THE ANCIENT YULETIDE CAROL' ✣ 65

Wassailing 66 ✣ *Carol Singing* 68 ✣ *'Silent Night'* 70 ✣ *'Good King Wenceslas'* 72 ✣ *'O Tannenbaum (O Christmas Tree)'* 74 ✣ *'Rudolph the Red-nosed Reindeer'* 76 ✣ *'Jingle Bells'* 78 ✣ *'White Christmas'* 79 ✣

FOREWORD

To all members of the human family who seek a better understanding and appreciation of their own and others' faiths.

All God's names are hallowed.
MARTIN BUBER

The celebration of Christmas is accompanied by numerous traditions and customs which have developed in many parts of the world over a long period of time. No other festival has produced such a wealth and variety of customs, and each one has its own fascinating story. This book explains how all the different customs started and what they mean.

Whichever way you celebrate Christmas, it is a season of good will. It is a time to try to renew bonds of affection and foster the spirit of giving; a time to plant joy in the hearts of people around you, especially those who are most deprived. The many lights we see decorating homes and trees at Christmas time are not just pretty decorations: they should remind us to spread the brightness of spirit which is so much needed in our world today.

'TIS THE SEASON TO BE JOLLY'

ADVENT

Advent is four weeks before Christmas. It starts either on St Andrew's Day or the Sunday nearest to it — known as Advent Sunday — and it ends on Christmas Eve.

The name Advent, from the Latin *adventus*, means the 'coming' or advent of Jesus Christ. This is most obviously the occasion of His birth, which is remembered and celebrated on Christmas Day. However, it can also refer to His 'second coming' when He is expected to judge the world on its 'Judgement Day'.

Advent was once a solemn time, a period of penitence. It has now totally changed in character. Young children in particular look forward to the 'coming' of Christmas. They are given colourful Advent calendars which they use to eagerly count the days until Christmas Day. Advent has become a happy and exciting adventure.

Fixing wreaths to the outside of the front door is a well-known custom during Advent, and is an expression of joyful anticipation.

'CHRIST'S MASS'

The word Christmas is derived from 'Christ's Mass', the first religious celebrations which honoured Jesus Christ's birth.

Interestingly, the Gospels do not indicate an actual date for this birth. In fact, to start with, 'Christ's Mass' was celebrated some time in April or May. There was an obvious clue for this choice. Remember St Luke's report that, at the time, shepherds were keeping watch over their flocks by night 'in the fields' (Luke 2:8)? This would have been most unlikely during winter, as sheep were kept indoors.

It was not until AD 350 that Pope Julius I designated December 25 as Christmas Day. He did so mainly to counteract the effect of the popular feast held in honour of Saturn – Saturnalia – which occurred at the time of the winter solstice. Many of the customs of Christmas merrymaking were similarly adopted from early pagan practices, and Christianised.

NOEL

Noël, the French word for Christmas, is derived from the Latin *dies natalis*, meaning 'birthday'. It became established in the English language through the popular carol, 'The First Noël'.

The word Noël has been the subject of fanciful folk etymology — interpretations that go far beyond the Latin root have been ascribed to it. For instance, Noël was said to derive from *nouvelles*, the French word for the (good) 'news', because this is what the birth of Jesus Christ brought to the world. Others recognised in Noël a corrupted rendering of the joyful claim that, with the saviour's coming, everything was 'now well'. A third interpretation suggests that Christmas was called Noël because, for those who accepted Jesus Christ as the Messiah, there would be 'no hell'.

XMAS

The spelling of Christmas as 'Xmas' comes from an ancient Greek practice.

In the Greek language, the letter 'x' — *shi* — was the initial letter of Xristos, meaning Christ. Early scribes were busy people and parchment was costly. They often shortened words to save time and money, and that is how they came to use just the letter X.

'Xmas' was retained even when these practical considerations no longer applied. Not only had it become traditional, but people believed, wrongly, that the 'X' represented St Andrew's cross. An even more significant reason, perhaps, was that Jesus Christ's name was regarded as too sacred to be written in full.

BOXING DAY

The day after Christmas is St Stephen's Day, named in honour of Christianity's first martyr. In Britain and the Commonwealth countries, however, it is known as Boxing Day.' This name has nothing to do with prize fights or pugilism — it actually does refer to a box.

Traditionally, a box containing a gift, or cash, was handed to postmen and tradesmen on this day, in recognition of 'services rendered' throughout the year. Like so many of our customs, this one started in ancient Rome where people exchanged presents during the festival of Saturnalia. The Church was unable to eradicate this custom, so they gave it a new, religious, meaning, saying that any material gift received had to be used for the spiritual benefit of the donor: to pay for special prayers or Masses offered on their behalf.

For instance, before a ship left port a priest would put an empty box on board, which was dedicated to the saint under whose protection the ship sailed. As a penance for any misdemeanours, seamen were expected to place contributions in the box, which was opened on the ship's homecoming. In return for the money collected, the priest then said Mass for the men. It was a kind of early 'Christ's Mass', and the box into which the offerings had been placed became known as the Christ's Mass Box. The money itself was distributed by the Church among the poor.

The box went on to become a symbol of charity and was given a permanent place in every church sanctuary. It was traditionally opened straight after the morning service on Christmas Day. The parish priest then distributed the money it contained among the needy on the following day. So, the day became known as Boxing Day. Most of these boxes were earthenware, in order to deter thieves. To open them, you had to break them.

This custom eventually became secularised. At one stage, apprentices were sent to call on their master's clients the day after Christmas, with boxes at the ready to collect tips! The boxes have been discarded, but the gifts are expected just as before — and not only by apprentices. Oddly enough, any such gratuity is still sometimes referred to as a 'Christmas box'.

THE PANTOMIME

Pantomimes are a key part of English Christmas celebrations. They are spectacular productions with lots of fun, jokes, songs and even commentaries on current affairs.

Paradoxically, these noisy performances go by a Greek name that describes complete silence! 'Pantomime', literally, means that 'all' (*pan*) is 'mime'. For thousands of years this was in fact the case, with not a single word being spoken or sung in a pantomime. Everything was expressed through gestures, dance and mime.

The version of the pantomime we know is only 200 years old. So different from its prototype, it nevertheless perpetuates one significant feature of pagan times: the reversal of roles. Men are always dressed as women, and women as men.

THE TWELVE DAYS OF CHRISTMAS

In AD 567, at the Council of Tours in France, the Church extended the period of celebrating Christmas to 12 days, from the nativity to Epiphany, the day when Jesus Christ manifested Himself to the world. According to the Julian calendar, Epiphany was the original Christmas Day celebrated by the Eastern Church, and it is still kept as such by the Armenian Church. It has also been suggested that the Church actually borrowed the idea of this twelve day period from the pagan celebration of the winter solstice, Saturnalia.

The 'twelve days of Christmas' was a very festive time, distinguished by exuberant, even riotous, behaviour. Activities included the appointment of a Lord of Misrule, or King of the Bean, the lighting of bonfires, pouring cider over apple trees and, not least, wassailing (about which more, later).

No doubt that now-famous folk song greatly contributed to the popularity of the idea of making Christmas last for longer than one day. This song, 'The Twelve Days of Christmas', became part of the traditional Twelfth Night party of the 16th and 17th centuries, when mince pies and iced cakes were eaten for the last time. The whole company would join in all twelve verses, repeating the text after a leader. As the verses became progressively longer — and therefore harder to remember — anyone making a mistake had to pay a forfeit. The task would be difficult enough when sober, and even more so after plenty of 'Christmas spirit' had been drunk!

On the 12th day of Christmas, my true love sent to me
12 lords a-leaping, 11 ladies dancing,
10 pipers piping, 9 drummers drumming,
8 maids a-milking, 7 swans a-swimming,
6 geese a-laying, 5 gold rings,
4 calling birds, 3 French hens,
2 turtle doves, and a partridge in a pear tree.

TWELFTH NIGHT

The 'Twelfth Night' after Christmas concluded the festive season.

In earlier times, this was the last opportunity for exuberance and revelry before people returned to their regular routine, so they used to spend the night with games, disguises and plays. Among the comedies often performed was Shakespeare's *Twelfth Night*. It was specifically written for this occasion and was first produced in 1602.

EPIPHANY

On January 6 – the Twelfth Day after Christmas – Christians observe the Feast of the Epiphany.

On this day the Magi, the three wise men from the East, are said to have arrived at Bethlehem with their gifts for the infant Jesus Christ. This was the first time that He was shown to the world, and this is what is commemorated at Epiphany. The name comes from the Greek *epiphania*, which means 'manifestation' or 'showing'.

It is commonly believed that the three Magi followed a star, and came to pay homage to the baby Jesus Christ. In fact, the original Gospels give no indication of the names or the numbers of the visitors; nor do they say, as is often claimed, that they were kings. These fanciful details were added much later on.

Tertullian of Carthage, who was converted to Christianity c.195 AD and who became a famous supporter of the early Church, said that the Magi were 'almost kings' (he used the Latin words *fere reges*). It was at least another 300 years before the Magi's royal status was claimed by quoting the Psalmist who spoke in Psalm 72:10, of far-off kings 'who shall bring presents' and 'offer gifts'.

Origen, a 3rd century Father of the Church and eminent biblical scholar, was the first to assert that the Magi were three in number. This was indicated in the Gospels, he claimed, by the three different gifts they carried — the gold, the frankincense and the myrrh. The claim that their names were Gaspar, Melchior and Balthasar comes from an even later date — in fact, it cannot be traced back any earlier than the 8th century.

According to a legend related by the 8th century English historian St Bede, Gaspar was a young man with a ruddy complexion, while Melchior was of a venerable age, white-haired and with a beard. Balthasar is described as dark-skinned and with a thick beard. Each of the three presents was given a symbolic meaning in terms of the life and death of Jesus Christ. Gold was a tribute to His royal status, frankincense symbolised His divinity as the son of God, and myrrh alluded to His death, being the chief ingredient used in the embalming of the dead.

Epiphany traditionally concludes the Christmas season. This is why it is still considered correct to leave Christmas decorations in place until then.

CHRISTMAS PARTIES AND PAPER HATS

Strangely, the custom of wearing colourful paper hats at Christmas parties and festive meals originated years ago. In those days many superstitions surrounded the sun, especially in relation to saving the sun – and, therefore, human life – from extinction. In early times, it was believed that evil forces constantly threatened the sun's survival. As evil could only be fought with evil, assuming the guise of the devil was therefore thought to drive away any real devils. Bizarre masks and hats were an essential part of such 'devil disguises'.

CHRISTMAS CARDS

The Christmas card was invented by Sir Henry Cole in 1843. He was a well-known London art dealer who aspired to improve the general public's taste. At his shop in Old Bond Street, he sold all kinds of beautiful *objets d'art.*

Nothing was too small or too trifling for Cole's aesthetic attention. He firmly believed that everyday things should be beautiful as well as useful. He came up with the idea of the first Christmas card, a simple yet attractive token of friendship which, he felt, would further enhance this special day.

Two factors are thought to have inspired Cole's endeavour. Firstly, he had the example of Valentine cards, which had been popular in England for almost a century. Also, towards the end of the winter term it was customary for pupils in English schools to produce 'Christmas pieces'. These were

large sheets of paper which the pupils decorated with colourful borders and headings, and then inscribed with Christmas greetings in their best copperplate. As well as being a charming expression of affection to the parents and teachers, such a piece also indicated a pupil's progress in the art of writing.

Cole commissioned a well-known artist, J. C. Horsley, a member of the Royal Academy, to design the picture for his first card, specimens of which can still be seen in museums and galleries. The picture was based on the common medieval artistic device of a triptych, a set of three illustrations. The central one depicted a jolly party of adults and children with plenty of food and drink – a subject that aroused severe criticism from the Temperance Movement at the time! Underneath the picture ran the seasonal greeting: 'Wishing a Merry Christmas and a Happy New Year to you'. Each side panel represented good works – the clothing of the naked and the feeding of the hungry.

Cole was well versed in the art of publicity and he did his utmost to popularise the new cards. However, for some unknown reason, his idea just did not catch on until 20 years later. By the 1860s, big stationery firms were producing thousands of Christmas cards and Cole's initial failure had become a tremendous success. During the next three

decades, British printers supplied 163,000 varieties of Christmas cards. These are now collected in 700 volumes, which weigh almost seven tonnes!

Cole was knighted in acknowledgment of his many services to the nation. He died in 1882, having lived to see and enjoy the enormous success of his original idea.

'DECK THE HALLS WITH BOUGHS OF HOLLY'

THE WREATH

The wreath traditionally displayed on the front door of a home during the weeks of Advent and the Christmas season once fulfilled a multiple role.

It was intertwined with red ribbons to express the festive spirit, while its evergreen leaves were symbolic of the everlasting life which Jesus Christ's birth promised to the faithful. The circular shape was a reminder of the crown of thorns placed on His head by the Roman soldiers when they ridiculed Him as the 'king of the Jews'. Yet another suggestion links the wreath with celebrations related to the god Bacchus, whose worshippers were thought to have worn circular ivy crowns.

Early on, the wreath also had a practical purpose. In a world full of fear and superstition, evergreen boughs were believed to protect a home from evil spirits, which were thought to be plentiful during this dark time of the year. During the Middle Ages the red berries of holly were believed to keep witches out of the home; this is why holly became the traditional and lucky evergreen for wreath-making.

BELLS

The jubilant ringing of church bells on Christmas morning celebrates the birth of Jesus Christ.

Legend has it that bells were rung for the hour before midnight on that first Christmas eve, warning the forces of darkness of the Saviour's imminent birth. At the stroke of midnight, their solemn knells changed into joyous pealing.

The sounding of bells served another purpose as well. Just as bells were tolled to announce the death of someone in the community, so they were rung to tell of the 'death' of the Devil brought about by the coming of Jesus Christ. The church bell was, therefore, also known as 'the Old Lad's Passing Bell', 'Old Lad' being a euphemism for Satan. The pealing of bells has also been assumed to chase away evil spirits, which are repelled by noise of any kind – even the clinking of glasses.

Bells of many types are a feature of the Christmas season. They can be heard on Christmas morning, and they are also used to decorate Christmas cards and the Christmas tree. Wassailers used to announce their presence by ringing a bell; so did Father Christmas, with jingling bells accompanying his sleigh's progress.

THE NATIVITY SCENE

The crib, representing the manger in which the baby Jesus Christ was laid after his birth in a stable in Bethlehem, has become a favourite Christmas decoration. For centuries it has been used to bring the Christmas story to life.

Francis of Assisi, who was renowned for his love of animals, instituted the custom of the nativity scene. After receiving permission from the Pope, he erected the first one during the Christmas of 1224 in a cave outside the Italian town of Greccio. It was not the modern type of crib or *crêche* (its alternate name from the Old French) nor was it a crafted model — but a live scene. A friend, John Velita, supplied Francis with a manger, straw and animals. It was a novel and eye-catching way to celebrate the memory of the child who was born in Bethlehem. When people gathered to view the spectacle, Francis stood in front of the manger and recited the Gospel relating to the scene; then he delivered a sermon.

Francis of Assisi's idea certainly caught the public's imagination. Today, nativity scenes with the figures of Joseph, Mary and the three wise men along with an ox and an ass, have become popular throughout the Christian world.

HOLLY

The evergreen holly symbolises eternal life. This shrub's most conspicuous features have long been associated with Jesus Christ. The bright red berries represent the drops of blood He shed on the cross; their colour also represented the burning love for God present in the hearts of the faithful. The prickly leaves remind us of the crown of thorns the Roman soldiers placed on Jesus Christ's head.

KISSING UNDER THE MISTLETOE

Kissing under the mistletoe, now a romantic and innocent practice, originated in the early belief that this plant, which stayed green even in winter, could produce and increase sexual power.

In some parts of the world mistletoe was regarded as being so potent that it could increase the productivity of the soil, be used as a fertility drug for cattle, and as a cure for impotence in humans. Although its fabled aphrodisiac role is now long forgotten, a vestige of it is retained in the romantic Christmas custom with which the plant is associated now.

The Druid priests of early Britain worshipped the mistletoe. A parasitic plant, it grew intertwined with the branches of oak trees, which were also objects of veneration for the Druids. Clad in white robes, Druid priests used to cut the 'golden bough' of the mistletoe with golden sickles and then distribute bunches of the plant to the faithful. The Druids believed that the mistletoe's magic potency extended far beyond just conferring fertility. It was thought to cure almost any disease, and was therefore known as 'all healer'. Sprigs fixed above doorways of homes were said to keep away

lightning and many kinds of evil. As the plant had no roots in the ground, it was imagined in these early times that it grew from heaven, which gave it all its wondrous qualities.

An old superstition had it that a girl who had not been kissed under the mistletoe would be barren. Today, kissing under the mistletoe is only an excuse to take innocuous liberties, but it began as part of sexual orgies conducted in honour of Saturn, and was part of a genuine attempt to guarantee fruitfulness. No wonder the early Christians tried — unsuccessfully! — to abolish the custom, and churches banned the plant from their precincts. One tradition demanded that a berry had to be removed from the bough for each kiss, so its usage was limited.

THE POINSETTIA

The poinsettia is named after Joel R. Poinsett, who served as the USA's first ambassador to Mexico, from 1825 to 1829. During that time he came to admire a beautiful indigenous plant with large scarlet leaves encircling small, greenish-yellow blossoms, which the Mexicans had adopted as their Christmas flower. He liked it so much that he sent specimens back to the USA, where they soon flourished.

A Mexican legend tells how the poinsettia became a Christmas flower. A poor peasant girl was anxious to bring a gift in honour of the Virgin Mary to the Christmas Eve service. She had nothing of value, though, so she went empty-handed. On her way to church she met an angel, who told her to pick some weeds. She did so and, with a heavy heart and a feeling of shame, placed them on the altar. Miraculously, they were transformed into the bright scarlet 'flowers'. Ever since, poinsettias have been popular decorations for churches and homes during the Christmas festival.

THE YULE LOG

Yuletide is an alternative name for the season of Christmas. This name was first used for a pre-Christian feast — the Scandinavian celebration of Juul — which was observed at the same time of year. The Juul, meaning a wheel, represented the annual (apparent) revolution of the sun. At Yuletide the sun was at its very lowest, but would, hopefully, come back. The yule log was a magical source of much-needed fuel for the sun, and subsequently symbolised the sun's light, warmth and life-giving power. Another story has an Anglo Saxon and Gothic origin for 'yule', which supposedly referred to the ale drunk at that time.

Christianity adopted the yule log and it became customary to place it on the hearth on Christmas Eve. It was kept burning there for at least twelve hours, its glow adding extra warmth to the home and enhancing the atmosphere of the festival. Strict rules had to be followed in everything pertaining to the log. It could never be purchased: it had to be received as a gift, be part of a tree grown on one's own property or just be picked up. It had to be kindled with a fragment of the previous year's log which had been specially preserved for this purpose, and its fire was never to be permitted to go out by itself.

'O CHRISTMAS TREE, O CHRISTMAS TREE'

THE TREE

The Christmas tree, with its green foliage, has its origins in very ancient beliefs in magic. At the time of the winter solstice, when all nature seemed dead, evergreen branches were thought to ensure the return of vegetation and new life. According to Norse mythology, evergreen trees represented the World Tree, whose branches and roots joined together heaven, earth and hell.

Trees figure in many cultures as symbols of enduring and renewed life, since the colour green is a universal emblem of immortality. For instance, the Egyptians used palm branches with 12 shoots as sacred expressions of the completion of the year. Palm branches were also carried during their funeral processions as symbols of life after death.

The Romans decorated their homes, temples and statues with foliage during the December festival of Saturnalia. This was a season of great goodwill towards all. Schools were closed. No battles could be fought. Punishment could not be inflicted on any criminal and distinctions of rank and class were put aside. The Jews also had a celebration that fell during this time — the Feast of Lights. For eight consecutive days an eight-branched candlestick would be lit in every Jewish home.

The early Christians realised it would be impossible to abolish all the old traditions, and so, wisely, retained the green tree and the burning lights — but gave them a new interpretation. In justification, they quoted the prophet Isaiah who had spoken of the 'righteous branch' and foreseen the day when 'the glory of Lebanon shall come unto you: the fir tree, the pine tree, and the box tree, to beautify the place of My Sanctuary'.

How the first modern Christmas tree came into being is related in numerous legends.

A Scandinavian story tells of the violent deaths of two lovers and a consequent occult occurrence: a beautiful tree grew out of the blood-soaked soil at the spot where the murder took place. Flaming lights miraculously appeared on it at Christmas time every year, and nothing could put them out.

For Germans, the tradition of the Christmas tree began with an incident that is said to have occurred when St Boniface arrived from England in AD 718 to convert the pagans.

He was determined to root out all that was heathen and, to this end, he cut down a sacred oak in the city of Geismar. To pacify the angry worshippers he planted a fir tree in its stead, and declared this to be the symbol of their new faith. It so happened that this event took place on Christmas Eve.

Martin Luther, the father of the German Reformation, has also been credited with the introduction of the modern Christmas tree. Returning home on a snowy Christmas Eve in 1517, he was deeply moved by the beauty of the glittering stars overhead. Wishing to describe this inspiring spectacle to his wife and children, he dug up a small fir tree and put it into the nursery. He then lit up its branches with candles, just as the starlit trees outside had appeared to him that cold winter night.

It took a long time for the tree to become part of Christmas celebrations in English-speaking countries. The first Christmas tree recorded in the USA was put up by Hessian soldiers in 1776. They were mercenaries hired from Prussia (now Germany) by King George III of England to fight in the Revolutionary War. The first English Christmas tree appeared at a children's party held at Queen Caroline's Court in 1821. German merchants based in Manchester had just introduced trees to that region, thus starting the trend.

Royalty was responsible for popularising the Christmas tree throughout the UK. Prince Albert, Queen Victoria's German-born husband, had a Christmas tree erected in Windsor Castle in nostalgic remembrance of his homeland. This royal example was soon copied by the general public, and the custom then spread throughout the world.

CANDLES

The custom of lighting candles at Christmas originates far back in time. Lighting candles was part of early sun worship: like bonfires, candles were lit in the depths of winter in an attempt to magically strengthen the weakened sun.

When the Church could not stamp out this ancient custom, it invested the lighting of candles with a new, and Christian, meaning. The candles were lit, so the Church taught, to symbolise the divine light that was believed to illuminate the world. According to another Christian tradition, candles were meant to recall the lights people lit in their windows at the time of Jesus Christ's birth, to let Joseph and Mary know that they would be welcome in their homes.

The lighting of candles has also been associated with that period in Irish history when the Catholic religion was banned. A Catholic family would signal when it was safe for a priest to come into their home to celebrate a clandestine Mass by placing a lighted candle in one window. In this way Christmas candles also pay silent tribute to people of all faiths who, in the face of persecution, remain loyal to their beliefs.

THE STAR

The star placed at the very top of the Christmas tree recalls the one seen by the three wise men 'in the East' at the time of Jesus Christ's birth, the star that 'went before them till it came and stood over where the young child was' (Matthew 2:1—12).

Several attempts have been made to identify this 'star of Bethlehem'. Some researchers have suggested that it was a comet with a fiery tail. In fact, Halley's comet has been cited as a possibility. It is visible every 76 years and would have been particularly brilliant in the eastern sky. Other astronomers have calculated that the planet Jupiter would have been rising, rather like a shining morning 'star', over Bethlehem in August, 2 BC. In the 17th century, the renowned astronomer Johannes Kepler referred to a specific conjunction of the planets Jupiter and Saturn in the constellation of Pisces which would have occurred in 7 BC. This was a most unusual phenomenon, and could easily have appeared to the naked eye as one great light.

In recent times, the star has been explained as a supernova which flared up at the time to an extraordinary brilliance and stayed bright for many weeks before fading away. However, as none of the dates for these planetary or astral oddities coincide with the traditional year of Jesus Christ's birth, the 'star of Bethlehem' remains a mystery.

TINSEL

The symbolism of light is behind the custom of decorating the Christmas tree with glittering tinsel. Light in all forms – fire, candles, even a flashing jewel – was thought to be magic enough to ensure that the forces of darkness would not have any power.

Christianity has added its own message, weaving a beautiful legend around the origins of tinsel. A poor widow was determined to give her large family a memorable Christmas, so the story goes, but all she possessed was a tree. She spent many hours decorating it and finally fell asleep, exhausted. Late that night, spiders wove webs all over the tree's branches. Then, to reward the widow's unselfishness, the Christ-child changed the spider webs into shining silver threads.

Legend also has it that, as a child, Jesus Christ once decorated a tree. He was assisted in this task by angels and, when their hair was caught on the branches as they departed, it turned into tinsel.

BAUBLES AND APPLES

The use of apples in some parts of the world to decorate trees stems from the apple's early associations with the Tree of Life in Paradise. According to popular belief, though the Bible never actually says so, this was an apple tree.

Baubles might be replicas of the fruit. Mainly, however, they are just colourful ornaments which contribute to the festive spirit in a home. They also reflect light, thus multiplying the effect of candles and lights.

GIFTS

The exchanging of Christmas presents can be traced back to an ancient Roman custom of gift-giving which was practised at Saturnalia, which also fell at this time of the year.

When this tradition was Christianised, it was said to relate to the gifts of gold, frankincense and myrrh that the Magi had carried with them from the East when they travelled to pay homage to the newborn Jesus Christ.

'THE GOOSE IS GETTING FAT'

THE TURKEY

For centuries, the boar's head and the fattened goose were the main course for an English Christmas dinner. The turkey was imported from the USA to Europe, reaching the UK in the 1520s. Once there, however, it soon 'gobbled up' the traditional English Christmas fare!

There were several reasons for turkey becoming so popular. For one thing, the bird was conspicuous by its bulk and patterned feathers, and it attracted further attention by the way it strutted about the farmyard — it almost asked to be served in honour of Christmas. Most of all, however, it was the delicious taste of its savoury and succulent meat that established the turkey as a popular and permanent feature of the Christmas table.

THE PUDDING

The Christmas pudding can be traced far back into the distant and pre-Christian past. In the freezing cold of the northern hemisphere the fields lay barren during winter. People were worried whether the land would provide them with the grain they needed to keep alive in the year to come. Therefore they tried to ensure the land's fertility by preparing a magical 'pudding'.

To begin with, this was simply wheat boiled in milk. Christianity adopted this cereal dish but suppressed or forgot all about its original magical significance, using the pudding for breakfast fare on Christmas Eve. Though this practice was eventually discontinued, the pudding was retained as a side dish to the meat course of the Christmas dinner. Gradually, it was enriched with the addition of other ingredients, such as eggs, prunes, and even chunks of meat. The pudding thus developed into a sort of meaty plum porridge, and was served in a tureen. Ultimately, the meat was again omitted to make the delicious sweet plum pudding we know today.

'FIRING' THE PUDDING

Lighting up the Christmas pudding with brandy-fed flames gives extra zest to both the eating of the pudding and the celebration. This fire is also pre-Christian in origin, recalling the fervent prayers and magic rituals aimed at helping the 'dying' sun in its fight for survival during the dark northern winter.

THE COIN IN THE PUDDING

An exciting moment during the Christmas dinner is finding out who the lucky person is whose portion of the pudding contains the coin. Children especially treasure this custom, even though the coin itself has little value.

The coin in the pudding might well be a remnant of the exuberant festivities once held on the very last day of the Christmas period, Twelfth Night. In memory of the three kings who are said to have arrived in Bethlehem at that time, a special mock 'king' would be chosen for that day only. Their rule was distinguished by turning everything topsy-turvy, and reversing every social and moral tradition. Servants were to be served by their masters and sexual indulgence abounded. Very appropriately, this person's title was 'the King of Misrule'.

Another name for this 'king for a day' was 'King of the Bean', based on the method by which he or she was chosen.

A bean was included in the mixture of a cake baked for the occasion. When the cake was broken up and its pieces distributed among the company, whoever found the hidden bean was crowned the 'King of the Bean'. This ancient ritual might well be the origin of our modern coin in the pudding.

Going much further back in time, a gruesome ceremony belonging to the pagan Saturnalia celebration could also be responsible for the custom. Then, the finding of the coin brought not pleasure but death. It was part of a barbaric lottery in which the 'winner' lost his life. The people back then believed that they needed the gods' aid to save themselves and the world from freezing to death — but the 'price' of this was a human life. This sacrifice would ensure the gods' help in preventing the sun 'standing still', the literal meaning of 'solstice'. At the same time, the sacrificed person's blood would magically fertilise the soil on which it fell to ensure its ability to produce crops in spite of the freezing conditions.

The only problem was how to decide who would be sacrificed! To this end, a lottery was devised so the gods themselves could choose. A coin was hidden in a pudding, and whoever found it was considered to be the divine choice for the sacrifice. Thankfully, all that remains of this original draw for death is the idea of the coin.

MINCE PIES

The mince pie was once a very significant part of Christmas fare; similarly, in days gone by its name once made more sense.

The mince pie was originally of oblong shape, with a crusty cover which was indented at the centre. The pie symbolised Jesus Christ's cradle. In fact, a small pastry doll — the figure of the Christ-child — used to be placed in the hollow.

This early mince pie was actually a meat pie, filled with minced lamb's tongue and mutton. On their return from the East, the medieval Crusaders brought highly prized spices with them which eventually replaced the meat in the pie, which also became round rather than oblong in shape.

Though its original symbolism has been forgotten and its name has actually become a misnomer, the mince pie remains one of the favourite treats of Christmas.

CHRISTMAS CAKE

The Christmas cake is a relatively recent addition to Christmas festivities, dating back only to the middle of the 19th century. It developed from the plum pudding; the contents were merely modified so that it would set solid.

THE STOLLEN

The universally popular Christmas treat known as the *Stollen* is of German origin. It is a kind of sweet bread, enriched with a variety of dried fruits and nuts and covered with icing sugar. Originally, families and bakeries treasured their special recipes for the *Stollen* they baked, and would not reveal their secret ingredients.

The *Stollen*, in its sugar coating, symbolises the baby Jesus Christ wrapped in swaddling clothes. The word itself refers to its shape, which is rather like a short 'prop' or 'post'.

CRACKERS

These are comparatively recent, dating back to the middle of the 19th century, and are said to be of French origin.

In their earliest form, in France, crackers were sweets or bon-bons enclosed in twists of coloured paper. An English pastrycook named Tom Smith saw these bon-bons while visiting Paris. On his return home, he copied the idea of a wrapper, but added other small gifts, as well as slips of paper inscribed with jokes, wise sayings or imaginative advice concerning the future. Small toys and paper hats were other surprise inclusions.

Smith's novel idea did not catch on at first. Then, on Christmas night 1846, as he sat in front of his fireplace with its crackling logs, he got the idea of imitating this sound. He did this by inserting a small explosive in the paper tube, which was set off with a bang by pulling from either side. This saw the birth of the popular and appropriately-named 'cracker'.

'HE SEES YOU
WHEN YOU'RE
SLEEPING'

SANTA CLAUS

The original Santa Claus was St Nicholas, a 4th century bishop of Myra, which was in Asia Minor, now part of Turkey. All that is known of him is that he was a man of great piety and compassion who had to suffer much persecution.

After his death St Nicholas became the subject of numerous legends. One story related how he restored life to three schoolboys who had been murdered. This deed made him the favourite of children. Other miracles attributed to him included rescuing shipwrecked sailors and calming a stormy sea. The stories grew in the telling and Nicholas became the patron saint of a variety of countries, places and people, particularly sailors and children.

From Turkey, St Nicholas' fame spread far and wide. The day of his death – December 6th – became his feast day. On its eve he was believed to visit homes and leave gifts for those children who put shoes outside the door or hung up stockings to receive them.

The Dutch, in particular, came to love the legend of Nicholas. In their language his name became *Sinter Klaas*. When Dutch settlers arrived in the USA in the 17th century they built their first church in New Amsterdam – the future

New York — in the saint's honour. The British eventually Anglicised his name, thus creating the modern Santa Claus. When Santa Claus also became known as Father Christmas, his visit was postponed to Christmas Eve. He was clad in red and white, which were thought to have been the colours of his vestment when he served as bishop of Myra.

Traditions vary concerning the way Santa Claus travels and how he visits homes. Some accounts have him walking, carrying his heavy sack. Others depict him riding a horse or in a coach. However, he is most often in a sleigh pulled by reindeer, and invariably gives his permanent address as the North Pole.

THE SLEIGH AND REINDEER

A father's wish to give his children a memorable Christmas story led to the idea of Santa Claus arriving in a sleigh pulled by eight reindeer.

The father was Dr Clement Clarke Moore, Professor of Oriental and Greek Literature at the New York General Theological Seminary and the author of many scholarly works. On a cold winter's night in 1822, two days before Christmas, he sat down with his two little daughters in front of a blazing fire in their New York home to read them a poem he had written. He had called it *A Visit from St Nicholas*. It portrayed Santa 'dressed all in furs from his head to his foot', with 'a bundle of toys flung on his back'. He had a broad face and a round belly 'that shook when he laughed like a bowl full of jelly'. Moore described his Santa as chubby and plump, travelling in a sleigh pulled by reindeer:

. . . when what to my wondering eyes should appear
But a miniature sleigh and tiny reindeer . . .
More rapid than eagles
His coursers they came
And he whistled and shouted and called them by name
'Now Dasher! Now Dancer!
Now Prancer! And Vixen!
On Comet! On Cupid!
On Donner and Blitzen! . . .
Now dash away! Dash away! Dash away all!'

Dr Moore never intended to publish his poem. A friend of the family who was very much taken with it asked for a copy. The following year she sent it – anonymously, and without informing Dr Moore – to a journal in Troy in the state of New York, where it was published in the Christmas edition.

Other papers reprinted the poem, making it even more popular. None, however, gave credit to its author. Dr Moore himself possibly felt that, as a professor of considerable standing, he should not admit that he had written it. Only in 1844 – 22 years after he had first read it to his children – did he acknowledge his authorship. He then included *A Visit from St Nicholas* in a collection of his poetry.

Meanwhile, Moore's figure of Santa travelling in a reindeer-pulled sleigh had caught the public's imagination. It became so popular that it was taken for granted. It is ironic that no one, except for a few experts, knows anything of the erudite work of the learned professor. His sole enduring legacy is the image of Santa he presented to the world in a jingle which he originally did not intend to publish!

FATHER CHRISTMAS

The picture of a pot-bellied, bearded and bell-ringing Father Christmas we know is of even more recent origin than Santa Claus. He was created by Thomas Nast, a North American cartoonist, in drawings he made for *Harper's Weekly* during a period of 20 years from 1863 onwards. He based the pictures on Clement Clarke Moore's poem, gradually developing Moore's small, fat, elf-like creature into the Father Christmas now known to all.

STOCKINGS

St Nicholas, so yet another story goes, was deeply concerned about three lovely sisters. They lived on the outskirts of a city and were desperately poor and destitute. The saint was determined to save the girls from their most likely fate — prostitution.

One night he went to their home and, unnoticed, dropped three pieces of gold through the smoke-hole (chimneys did not exist at that time). The coins did not fall onto the hearth as he had expected, but into the sisters' stockings, which had been hung up near the fire to dry. Nothing could describe their happiness when they found the money in the morning. People have hung up Christmas stockings ever since, hoping to receive similarly pleasant surprises.

WHY THE CHIMNEY?

The chimney would seem to be the very last point of entry for Santa to choose! Apart from possibly getting his rotund body stuck in the narrow passage, the soot would ruin his outfit!

The idea of entering a home via the chimney dates from prehistoric times, when people actually dwelt underground. The smokehole — which was later replaced by the chimney — doubled as the entrance and the exit. This explains why, in present-day French, the words for both 'chimney' (*cheminée*) and 'path' (*chemin*) have the identical root, just as the Italian *cammino* communicates both meanings.

'TROLL THE ANCIENT YULETIDE CAROL'

WASSAILING

At one time the singing of Christmas carols was known as 'wassailing'. In particular, this term applied to the custom of a group of people, mainly children, going from house to house and stopping in front of each to render a carol, in the hope of receiving a reward.

The word 'wassail' dates back to pre-Christian days and practices. Derived from the Anglo Saxon *was hale* – 'be thou hale' – it expressed a wish for good health. This festive season toast was traditionally offered with a drink, usually a concoction of hot ale, roasted apples, sugar and spices. The blend was sometimes further enriched with eggs and cream, when it was known as 'lamb's wool'.

The well-wisher did not drink alone! The beautifully decorated wassail bowl was passed from hand to hand, so everyone in the household could share the toast in the spirit of true fellowship. After each sip, those partaking in the toast were expected to top up the bowl.

Indeed, great care was taken to ensure that the wassail bowl remained full throughout the entire festive season, from Christmas Eve to Twelfth Night, thus ensuring the continuity of good cheer.

These verses are typical of many of the early wassail songs:

Wassail, wassail, wassail syng we
In worship of Christ's nativity.

To begin with, the idea of wassailing went far beyond merely fostering goodwill. It had more to do with people's concern to see nature renew itself after the harsh winter months. Wassailing was believed to magically bestow fertility on the recipient, whether it was a man, a tree or a beast. For instance, fruit trees were toasted with the wassail bowl so that they would bear well in the coming season. This was most important in the case of apple trees, where a good crop would mean plenty of cider for the next year's wassailing!

CAROL SINGING

The idea of singing at Christmas time stems from the thought that the angels sang when they appeared to the shepherds at Bethlehem to announce Jesus Christ's birth.

The present-day meaning of a carol, however, is far removed from its original one. A carol was once a secular dance which was performed at any time of the year. People held hands and formed a ring and, as they circled around, they joined in song.

The configuration of the participants in this 'ring-dance' reminded onlookers of a coronet — *corolla* in Latin — so they called it a 'carol'. The name was later transferred from the dance to the song itself. By the 16th century, carols were sung only at Christmas time. The subject of the songs also came to relate exclusively to Christmas.

Another development followed. For some time Christmas carols were sung only in church, and only by the bishop and the clergy. But carols rapidly became popular amongst the general public and were soon sung in the streets and other public places. They dealt with the theme of Christmas, not just with the subject of Jesus Christ's birth, in the most varied of ways.

‘SILENT NIGHT’

This favourite Christmas hymn originated by accident. It was created for an emergency, on the spur of the moment, and owes its existence to . . . church mice!

On Christmas Eve 1818, Father Josef Mohr, the priest of the Austrian village of Oberndorf, was preparing his church for the midnight Mass. To his consternation, he discovered that the organ was out of order. Looking for the cause, he found that part of its leather bellows had been eaten away by mice. Time was too short to have the damage repaired.

Father Mohr felt that the service would lose much of its beauty and warmth if there were no music. Something had to take the place of the organ. He had written a Christmas poem which he now took to Franz Gruber, the local schoolmaster, who was also an amateur composer and, like himself, played the guitar. Mohr asked him whether he could quickly set this

poem to music so that it would be ready that night. He should do so for two solo voices to be accompanied by guitars. Gruber gladly obliged. It took him only a few hours to compose the tune of 'Silent Night, Holy Night', which was sung for the first time on the very night of its rapid composition by the two men in that little village church.

'Silent Night' captivated the hearts of many Christians, far beyond Oberndorf. The renowned Zillertal Choir sang the hymn at recitals all over the country, making it popular nationwide and, eventually, throughout Europe. Almost 100 years later, Bing Crosby gave it world fame.

'GOOD KING WENCESLAS'

This popular Christmas carol was written by John Mason Neale, a 19th century Anglican theologian and renowned hymnologist.

He 'borrowed' its catchy tune — which is chiefly responsible for its extraordinary popularity throughout the English-speaking world — from a 13th century secular spring dance! The 'King Wenceslas' to whom he dedicated the carol was actually a 10th century Bohemian prince who was hardly remembered in his own country, and had certainly never been heard of in Britain. For the carol's story, Neale made use of a medieval tale he had come across which told of Wenceslas' kindness. Little is otherwise known about this royal figure; he was killed in AD 929 as part of a plot to put his own brother in power.

In spite of the antiquity of both the tune and the tale, the carol's social message could not be more up to date. It speaks of the duty of the well off to show concern and compassion for the needy, to look after the poor and dispossessed:

Therefore, Christian men, be sure,
Wealth or rank possessing,
Ye who now will bless the poor
Shall yourselves find blessing.

'O TANNENBAUM (O CHRISTMAS TREE)'

With the evergreen Christmas tree having its origins in German soil, it would seem only appropriate for a German to have created the carol dedicated to it.

According to one tradition this person was Ernst Anschütz, an elderly teacher in the city of Leipzig. However, his work was prompted by circumstances far removed from the traditional Christmas spirit of peace and harmony.

Just before Christmas 1824, Anschütz had been greatly upset by a heated argument he had had with the headmaster of his school. The quarrel was weighing heavily on his mind as he made his way home, when he caught sight of Christmas trees being offered for sale. Somehow, this calmed his agitation. Was it not wondrous how this tree kept its green foliage, even during the harshest of winters? Perhaps it reminded him of how he, too, should be able to preserve his peace of mind during difficult times. Inspired, he sat down and leafed

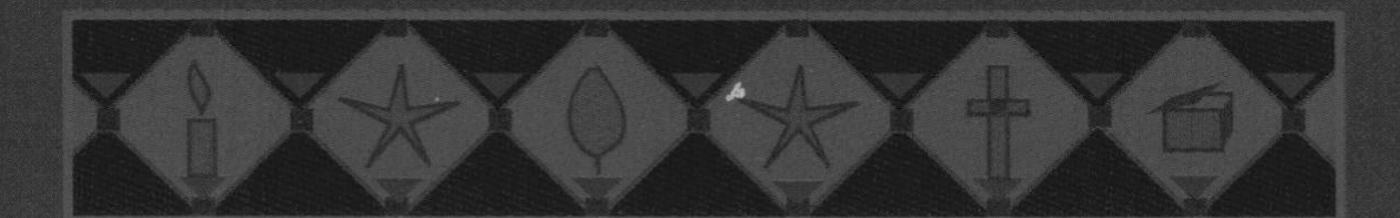

through a collection of folksongs by the Berlin composer August Zarnack. His attention was caught by a love song about a Christmas tree, and he lost no time converting it into the popular 'O Tannenbaum'.

Actually, the tune itself dates back to a 12th century Latin drinking song written by Walter de Mapes, a deacon at Oxford.

'RUDOLPH THE RED-NOSED REINDEER'

Every Christmas season the mail order store of Montgomery Ward, in Chicago, USA, used to distribute a colouring book for children as a free gift and advertisement. Until 1939, the firm obtained these books from a local manufacturer. In that year, however, the management decided that Montgomery Ward had all the facilities necessary to produce them themselves. This would not only save the firm a lot of expense, but would create an opportunity to present the books in a new form.

Robert (Bob) May, a 35 year-old employee working in the copy department, was given the task of putting together the colouring book. It was suggested that he create some new, lovable creature, similar to the popular 'Ferdinand the Bull'. Unfortunately, this job came at the worst possible time for May. He was deeply worried about his wife, who was terminally ill, and the medical bills had put him into great debt.

Despite his anguish, he accepted the job, deciding that his book would contain a story and pictures which gave a message of hope to people like himself who were facing problems. That is how he came to create the reindeer called Rudolph which pulled Santa Claus' sleigh. Rudolph's shiny red nose made other animals laugh at him, but this very defect was to prove an advantage. Like the strong headlight of a car, Rudolph's nose could penetrate the densest fog, guiding Santa to those who lived in dark, isolated and lonely places.

The boss rejected May's idea at first, but May persisted. Remembering the saying 'One picture is worth a thousand words', he asked Denver Gillen, a friend in the art department, to draw the reindeer he imagined. He resubmitted 'Rudolph with the red nose' — and this time his boss was enchanted.

When May's colouring book appeared the following Christmas, it immediately became a hit. Children lapped up the story of Rudolph, and the first print run of 3 million copies was quickly followed by many more. In 1949 Johnny Marks wrote the song, 'Rudolph the Red-nosed Reindeer' which, with its catchy tune and a first rendition by Gene Autry, was to become so popular.

'JINGLE BELLS'

James S. Pierpont was a popular American composer. He wrote the words and music of 'Jingle Bells', no doubt one of the most loved of all Christmas songs, in 1857.

Pierpont was a member of a staunch Unitarian Church family, and his father was a minister. It is no wonder, therefore, that he first composed his famous ditty — originally entitled 'One Horse Open Sleigh' — for a local Sunday school entertainment.

Its catchy tune was soon taken up by Christmas revellers who, early on, often accompanied the chorus with the jingling of glasses.

‘WHITE CHRISTMAS’

This lovely modern Christmas song was written in 1942 by Irving Berlin. He was a Jewish immigrant to the USA from Russia, where his father had been a cantor in a synagogue.

Out of Irving's 900 compositions, this was undoubtedly the most successful. He composed it for the film ‘Holiday Inn’, a musical which starred Bing Crosby and Fred Astaire. ‘White Christmas’ received the well-deserved Academy Award for Best Song of 1942, and the sale of its sheet music has never been surpassed by any other single song.